NORTH LONDON
27
RAILWAY

NATIONAL RAILWAY MUSEUM, YORK · SCIENCE MUSEUM, LONDON

NORTH LONDON RAILWAY

A PICTORIAL RECORD

LONDON   HER MAJESTY'S STATIONERY OFFICE

ACKNOWLEDGEMENTS

The writers would like to express their indebtedness to Messrs A. P. Hancox and L. H. J. Ward for their authoritative assistance in the preparation of this book and to *The Railway Magazine* for the information on which the map (pages xviii–xix) is based. Map by Brian P. Elkins.

Designed by HMSO Graphic Design

ISBN 0 11 290273 1

FRONTISPIECE

A group of staff at Bow Works posed in front of 4-4-0T No. 72, in shop grey livery. This engine was built at Bow in 1894. Mr Henry J. Pryce, the Locomotive Superintendent, is standing immediately below the locomotive number plate. The headgear appears to denote the status of the staff. Heads of departments wore top hats or 'Derbies', foremen used bowler hats and the footplate staff and guards had more modest caps.

The North London Railway ran their engines in shop grey for a period when new or after rebuilding.

COVER ILLUSTRATION: FRONT

An historical reconstruction of Dalston Junction at the turn of the century. Specially commissioned for this album, this view from the southern end shows the passenger and goods traffic that epitomized the daily routine of the North London Railway. The standard passenger train of twelve four-wheel coaches, headed by 4-4-0T locomotive No. 70, is pulling away from the platform, bound for Broad Street. On the Poplar line, an 0-6-0T, No. 17, is hauling a mixed freight train through to one of the LNWR goods depots near Broad Street.

The illustration is by Lyn D. Brooks and based on Ordnance Survey maps of the period; the North London Railway collection of the National Railway Museum and modern site photography by George L. Pring.

COVER ILLUSTRATION: BACK

North London Railway Armorial Device
Although the garter is inscribed North London Railway, the device represents the original title East & West India Docks & Birmingham Junction Railway. The top left quarter depicts an anchor bearing a shield emblazoned with a lion rampant, which represents the East India Dock. The shield of the City of Birmingham is on the top right, while the one on the bottom left is that of the City of London. The bottom right depicts the entrance to the West India Import Dock, which was demolished in 1932.

LIST OF ILLUSTRATIONS

FRONTISPIECE
Staff at Bow Works, in front of 4-4-0T No. 72, at Devons Road

PAGES XVIII–XIX
Map showing the development of the NLR.

PLATES

HISTORICAL DEVELOPMENT

The North London Railway (NLR) was incorporated as the East & West India Docks & Birmingham Junction Railway on the 26th August 1846, but adopted its more familiar title in 1853. This name survived until formal absorption of the company on 1st January 1922 by the London & North Western Railway (LNWR), which had in fact worked the line since 1st January 1909. There had always been strong administrative links between the NLR and the LNWR. The NLR Secretary had his office at Euston, rather than at Broad Street, and many of the LNWR directors sat on the NLR Board. The reference to Birmingham in the North London Railway's original title stemmed from the fact that the eight-mile line was originally regarded as the link between Chalk Farm on the London & Birmingham Railway (L & BR) and the docks at Poplar on the River Thames. The L & BR was one of the three constituents of the London & North Western Railway when the latter was formed in 1846.

Originally envisaged as a freight-only line, the North London Railway carried passengers from the opening day, since it passed through several prosperous suburbs of Victorian London, such as Canonbury and Hackney. The first section of the line to be opened was from Bow Junction to Islington, and a frequent passenger service was provided from Fenchurch Street Station to Islington by means of running powers over the London & Blackwall and the Eastern Counties Railways via Bow Junction. The line to Hampstead Road (Chalk Farm) was completed in January 1852.

Access to Kew was soon gained via the North & South Western Junction Railway (N & SWJR) which had been opened in February 1853. This provided for through goods traffic between the London & South Western Railway (LSWR) at Kew, and the LNWR, using a connection near what was later to become Willesden Junction. NLR passenger trains were run non-stop from Hampstead Road over LNWR rails to Kew, crossing the LNWR main line on the level at the junction.

Richmond (LSWR) was reached in 1858, trains being reversed over LSWR lines at Kew and again at Barnes. Later, in 1869, the access to Richmond was improved by use of the LSWR line from Acton Junction via Gunnersbury. The N & SWJR came under North London

Management in about 1860, although in 1871 it was leased to the LNWR, Midland and NLR, with the proviso that the North London should continue to provide the passenger service.

A branch from South Acton to Hammersmith and Chiswick was opened during 1857–8, although it was scarcely justified in view of the limited traffic potential. In order to do away with the congestion caused by the crossing of the LNWR main line on the level, the LNWR promoted the building of the Hampstead Junction Railway from a junction with the NLR at Camden Town to a junction with the N & SWJR at Old Oak. This line crossed the LNWR main line by a bridge at the station now named Willesden Junction. A spur was also provided to connect with the LNWR at Harlesden. After this line had been opened in January 1860, it was used by North London trains to Richmond and Kew.

In later years alterations were carried out at Willesden Junction to facilitate the interchange of freight. A junction and spur were put in to connect the North London with the West London Railway and Kensington (Addison Road). This enabled the LNWR to build exchange sidings for goods traffic from the LSWR, as well as from the Midland and Great Western Railways which had junctions at Acton Wells.

PASSENGER SERVICES

Such was the rapid development of passenger services on the North London that the desirability of a terminus situated in the City soon became apparent. This was opened at Broad Street on 1st November 1865, having cost approximately £1 million. (See plate 1.) It was located at the end of a branch off the original line via a triangular junction at Kingsland. Within ten years, work had to start on re-arranging and enlarging the terminus, and further extensions were carried out during 1890–91, as a result of which the original three platforms and four tracks had increased to a total of eight. (See plates 2–6.)

The several stations on the NLR route were very close together, being on average only about three minutes travelling time apart. Those originally built around 1850 were constructed of wood, but about twenty years later several, notably Camden Road, Caledonian Road & Barnsbury, Highbury & Islington, Canonbury, Hackney and Bow, were rebuilt in stone to the designs of E. H. Horne. They were designed in Venetian-Gothic style, unique in British railway architecture, and were constructed of white Suffolk brick, Portland stone and terra cotta.

The 1890s saw North London passenger operations at their height. In addition to the long-established Kew and Richmond service, the NLR had enjoyed from 1875 running powers over the Great Northern Railway (GNR) lines to High Barnet and New Barnet. Under this agreement, the NLR received a proportion of the through fares and a fixed sum per train mile over the GNR. The Great Northern had hoped to be able to use Broad Street station in addition to the Metropolitan Railway's City terminus at Moorgate, but this was blocked by the all-powerful LNWR. Soon the NLR operated a good half of the GN suburban services, running over 31 miles of Great Northern track, which included working the Enfield and Alexandra Palace branches. For a relatively short period the NLR services over the GN main line extended as far north as Hatfield but these were soon discontinued, for reasons unknown.

In East London the NLR also operated services over the London, Tilbury & Southend Railway (LT & S), maintaining a shuttle service between Plaistow and Bow until 1915. During holiday periods North London 4-4-0Ts and trains appeared at Southend by working over the LT & S.

By 1900 the North London Railway had physical connections with the Great Northern, Great Eastern, Great Western, London & North Western, London & South Western, Midland and Metropolitan District railways. Over these concerns it enjoyed running powers covering approximately 50 miles (mainly over the GNR), compared with its own route mileage of only 14 miles 20 chains. These many connections enabled traffic to be conveyed between all the main lines terminating in London, with the exception of the Great Central Railway which did not reach the capital until the turn of the century. During the early 1900s NLR passenger trains ran approximately 2 million miles each year, and freight trains approximately 500,000 miles.

At the turn of the century there were more daily arrivals at Broad Street station than at Euston and Paddington combined, and in this

respect the NLR terminus was exceeded only by Liverpool Street and Victoria. Between 9 and 10 am seventy-one passenger trains entered and left Broad Street on a normal weekday, the daily total being 794, involving the movement of an average of 85,000 passengers, while on special occasions no fewer than 210,000 had been handled. Large numbers of workmen were conveyed who travelled 3rd class at a standard return fare of 2d (slightly less than 1p) between any two North London stations, a system which was introduced in 1875.

TICKETS & REVENUE

On the North London Railway a simple but highly effective system was employed in order to ensure collection of the correct fare. From 1873 each station on the system was allocated a number (previously capital letters had been used) which was printed on all tickets valid to that particular station. Stations opened after this date were designated by a number with a letter 'A' suffix. Thus all the tickets given up at a particular station should bear the latter's specific number. A full list of station names and numbers is given opposite.

The use of the 2d flat rate fare for workmen enabled the North London to introduce the first automatic ticket issuing machines in the country. Machines were later installed at Broad Street in 1900 (see following page). North London Railway revenue reached a peak in 1900 after which electric tramway competition seriously affected receipts. This is clearly indicated in the financial returns given opposite, which must have prompted the 'takeover' by the LNWR in 1909.

North London Railway stations and their Ticket Code Numbers

1	Broad Street	17	Kentish Town
2	Shoreditch	18	Gospel Cak
3	Haggerston	19	Hampstead Heath
4	Dalston Junction	20	Finchley Road & Frognal
4A	Mildmay Park	20A	West End Lane
5	Canonbury	21	Brondesbury
6	Highbury & Islington	21A	Brondesbury Park
7	Caledonian Road & Barnsbury	22	Kensal Rise
		23	Willesden Junction
7A	Maiden Lane	24	Acton
8	Camden Town	24A	South Acton
9	Chalk Farm	25	Hammersmith & Chiswick
		26	Kew Bridge
10	Hackney	27	Gunnersbury
11	Homerton	28	Kew Gardens
12	Victoria Park	29	Richmond
13	Old Ford		
14	Bow		
15	South Bromley		
16	Poplar		

Year	Total Revenue £	Total Expenditure £	Balance Available for Dividend £	% Dividend Consolidated on stock
1875	389,442	182,533	122,505	6
1880	457,978	213,802	152,970	7½
1885	481,502	227,298	156,647	7½
1890	502,349	237,558	163,876	7½
1895	500,135	267,980	142,903	6¾
1900	559,419	322,451	152,428	7¼
1905	514,836	330,227	103,038	4¾
1908	463,066	301,053	80,663	3½

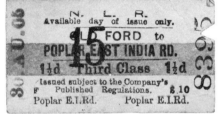

x

RIGHT Automatic machine, manufactured by the Sweetmeat Automatic Delivery Co Ltd, for the issue of workmen's tickets. Note the two separate slots for two pennies. These were among the earliest automatic ticket issuing machines in the country. In 1900, workmen's tickets between any two North London stations cost 2d return. The return half of the ticket was a different colour for each day of the week. In 1898, these machines were in use at Hackney, Homerton, Victoria Park, Old Ford, Bow and, in the previous year, 2,328,168 tickets of this sort were issued. Homerton needed two machines, the other four stations had one each.

THE RESULTS OF INTEGRATION

After the LNWR had taken over the working of the North London, it was able to take advantage of Broad Street's situation in the City of London. A special businessman's express was instituted between Broad Street and Wolverhampton via Birmingham. The inaugural run was made on 1st February 1910, and for the service the LNWR built a special dining car which was extremely spacious and luxurious. In addition, lady typists were available on the train and could take down dictation en route. However, the service was not a total success and the northbound train ceased to run after 13th July 1914, and the southbound after 22nd February 1915. Although the 'Precursor' 4-4-0 was then the standard LNWR passenger locomotive type south of Crewe, these were too heavy for the approaches to Broad Street and so the smaller 'Renown' class, initially No. 1918 *Renown* itself, was employed.

Although electrification had been considered by the North London Railway itself in 1904, the 1909 working arrangement with the LNWR permitted the latter to modify its own electrification proposals which were originally to have involved the construction of a new underground station beneath Euston Station. Instead, the route into Broad Street was electrified, work being initiated in 1911 on a four-rail 630 volt dc system. An additional (and final) platform (No. 9) was installed outside the western wall at Broad Street in 1913, and Platforms 5 to 9 were equipped with conductor rails. Delayed by the First World War, electric services between Broad Street and Richmond began on 1st October 1916. Broad Street station suffered some damage during the course of a Zeppelin raid, on 8th September 1915, which also disrupted the approaches to neighbouring Liverpool Street.

The LNWR, having absorbed the NLR in 1922, itself became a part of the London Midland & Scottish Railway (LMS) the following year, when the Great Northern Railway similarly became a part of the London & North Eastern Railway. As a result of this, LMS 0-6-0Ts could be seen working over the LNER main line as far north as Potters Bar. Additional competition now existed in the form of buses and the electric tube. Even so, the now obsolete North London four-wheeled carriages, unheated and gas-lit, remained in use until the 1930s.

Eventually, in 1930–32, the LMS constructed seven sets of special bogie passenger stock for the Alexandra Palace and certain other services. Apart from the provision of three classes of accommodation (2nd class having otherwise virtually disappeared by this time), they were in all essentials identical to normal LMS suburban coaches of that period.

In 1940 Broad Street station was put out of action for several days following a heavy air attack. After this the appearance of LMS locomotives working over the LNER main line ceased, and after the war ended LNER locomotives and trains worked out of Broad Street to Hertford North and Welwyn Garden City.

Following nationalisation of the railways in 1948, some main line services to Peterborough operated from Broad Street on summer Saturdays during 1950 and 1951 in order to relieve severe congestion on the approaches to Kings Cross. Latterly diesel-worked, the last remaining services over the former GNR suburban lines emanating from Broad Street ceased with the coming of the Kings Cross inner suburban electrification in November 1976. By 1968 only 9000 passengers each day were using Broad Street, which at the time of writing (1978) is threatened with extinction with the redevelopment of the adjacent Liverpool Street terminus, into which the former's residual services will be diverted.

OPERATING PRACTICES

Despite the density of its passenger operations the North London Railway had a good safety record, there being only one fatal accident throughout its entire existence. This occured at Old Ford on 28th January 1882 when a wagon running in a coal train was forced by a broken drawbar into a passenger train, killing five people. There were inevitably lesser contretemps from time to time, as indicated by plates 46 and 47, but the North London Railway was extremely safety conscious.

As early as January 1860, the NLR made use of the first effective signal interlocking device in this country, at Kentish Town cabin. On the NLR signalling came within the responsibility of the Locomotive Department from 1883 and further safety devices were evolved jointly by two successive Locomotive Superindendents, J. C. Park and H. J. Pryce.

Their main contribution was the provision of a train protection bar in each platform road at Broad Street (discernible in plate 2), which locked the inner home signal at danger while a train was standing in the platform on the bar. Between Camden Town and Broad Street separate signal boxes were provided to operate the fast and slow lines and these were manned continuously in three eight-hour shifts.

The North London Railway was the first British line to establish the everyday use of the continuous brake in 1855. Having experimented with numerous patterns of brake, Clark's chain brake was selected as standard from 1866 until superseded in 1873 by the Clark and Webb type. The latter was soon to fall into great disrepute on the LNWR, which had pioneered it, and in 1891 automatic vacuum brakes had to be adopted by the NLR in order to comply with Board of Trade regulations.

Comparatively little goods traffic originated on the North London Railway itself, which in American parlance would be described as being a 'bridge carrier.' Its great virtue lay in conveying large quantities of freight across London from one of the big main line companies to another, as well as imports to and from the Docks. One set of Docks, those at Poplar, were actually owned by the North London Railway and covered a total area of 28 acres, inclusive of goods warehouses, and contained 14 miles of sidings. All machinery was operated by hydraulic power, there being four accumulators at 700 p.s.i., charged by six pairs of compound pumping engines. There was a total of twenty three cranes and hoists, including a 30-ton quay crane. Forty capstans, eight coal-tipping machines and a swing bridge across the harbour entrance were provided. Hydraulic pressure was also utilized for special fire appliances which covered the warehouses, in addition to which the LNWR, GNR, and Great Western (GWR) also used it (by agreement) for the lifting equipment in their own neighbouring warehouses. (See plates 48–51.)

LOCOMOTIVES

To handle its very heavy passenger and freight services, the NLR operated a fleet of locomotives which was numerically quite large in relation to its low route mileage. Early locomotives were principally 2-4-0 and 0-4-2 tank engines. In 1854 the North London Railway appointed William Adams as its first Locomotive Superintendent. Born in Limehouse in 1823, he was the son of the Resident Engineer of the East & West India Docks. Before coming to the North London Railway at the early age of 31, Adams had already enjoyed a varied career which included a spell with the Royal Sardinian Navy. On taking up his appointment on the NLR, Adams wasted no time in establishing a works a Bow Junction for building and repairing locomotives, carriages and wagons. These works were located on both sides of the main line, and ultimately covered a total area of 31 acres. (See plates 9–19.) As a result, from 1863 the North London Railway was completely self-sufficient with regard to the manufacture of locomotives and rolling stock, an unusual situation on such a relatively short railway. Bow Works continued to repair steam locomotives until well into the 1950s, and finally closed to wagon repairs during the 1960s. The first locomotive to be built at Bow Works was an inside-cylinder 4-4-0 tank engine (No. 43) (see plate 22). This was developed from similar types produced by Robert Stephenson & Co. in 1855 (see plate 20) and Slaughter Gruning & Co. in 1861 (see plate 21). These all have distinctive short-wheelbase outside-framed bogies, but in those engines built from 1865 Adams introduced a longer wheelbased bogie of his own design, which he patented. (See plate 23.) This allowed spring-controlled lateral movement for the central pivot, an idea which ultimately attained worldwide adoption.

From 1868 the 4-4-0 tank engines built at Bow had outside cylinders, a basic format which remained in production until 1907, resulting in a type which predominated on the NLR passenger services for almost half a century. Plate 26 shows the original Adams design of 1868, and plate 27 the ultimate development by H. J. Pryce. The locomotives built by Adams had open cabs, polished brass domes, copper-capped chimneys, and they were styled in a most ornate green livery. Adams' successor from 1873, J. C. Park, introduced during the 1880s a sombre black livery reminiscent of the LNWR, and he also began to enclose the cabs. Despite the latter development, the coal bunkers on NLR locomotives always remained within the cabs. Their limited capacity for fuel was perhaps a further incentive to economy on a line on which, it has been claimed, low coal consumption came before punctuality. The drivers made much use

of falling gradients with the steam shut off. The last surviving NLR 4-4-0T, No. 6 of 1894, was set aside by the LMSR in 1928 for preservation, but was cut up four years later. However, we still have a very good idea of how these locomotives appeared, because a one-eighth scale model of No. 60 was constructed at Bow Works in 1889, at a cost of at least £1000 for display at the Paris Exhibition of that year. For many years subsequently it was displayed at Broad Street station where it was actuated by a 'coin in the slot'. It can now be seen in the National Railway Museum, and is probably one of the most authentic locomotive models ever made.

In 1900 NLR passenger trains made an average of 7000 stops each day, running over a route which included severe gradients (a maximum of 1 in 60 at Haggerston falling to Dalston Junction) and sharp curves. Not surprisingly, the stresses and strains were great in the 4-4-0Ts, which normally came in for heavy renewal every fifteen years or so. Boilers and/or frames would be replaced and the latest refinements in such details as brakes would be incorporated. At times there was very little distinction between what was regarded (usually for accountancy purposes) as a new engine and what was simply a so-called 'rebuild' (see plates 24, 25). As a result the history of the numerous NLR 4-4-0Ts is extremely complicated.

Rather more straight-forward were the thirty sturdy 0-6-0 tank locomotives first introduced by J. C. Park in 1879 to operate the freight services (see plates 27 and 29). With their short rigid wheelbase and outside cylinders, they were notoriously rough riding. Even in the late 1950s one or two were still to be seen working down to Poplar. The last survivor, and strangely only the second example to be built, lasted until 1960 on the Cromford & High Peak line in Derbyshire, and is now preserved by the Bluebell Railway in Sussex. After the LNWR takeover, several of the 4-4-0Ts also travelled far afield, turning up in such unlikely places as Llandudno Junction and Carnforth.

ROLLING STOCK

Bow Works built a variety of goods wagons, on a standard design of underframe, which were typical of their period. Representatives are illustrated in plates 32–36. Of greater interest was the NLR passenger stock, which was exclusively of the four-wheeled variety throughout the railway's independent existence (see plates 33–37). These were made up into block trains of varying length (see plate 32) by use of single link couplings, with buffers at one end only, a method evolved by William Adams. This reduced the distance between adjacent carriages from the conventional 4 feet or so to only 1 foot, in order to accommodate the maximum number of vehicles at platforms of restricted length. In 1862, the NLR was also the first railway in Great Britain to introduce coal-gas lighting in its carriages, an idea pioneered by the Dublin & Kingstown Railway four years earlier. The gas was stored in large flexible containers, or 'gas bags', which occupied a large part of the guard's and luggage vans. In later years the use of these was discontinued, and steel gas cylinders were fitted to each carriage on the underframe, making them self-contained. In such cases the space left unoccupied in the long type vans was then converted into two additional 3rd class compartments. The gas containers were regularly replenished via flexible connections when the trains were standing in Broad Street station. (See plate 2.)

For its passenger stock, the North London Railway adopted a livery of varnished teak, a sensible if austere style for that period having regard for the need to keep the coaches clean in a grimy industrial environment. Just how attractive this finish can appear is illustrated by the NLR Directors' Saloon, designed and constructed by William Adams at Bow Works in 1872, which is now preserved in the National Railway Museum. (See plate 38.)

In 1910 the Wolverton carriage works of the LNWR built some four-wheeled stock especially for the North London services (see plate 39). Subsequently some of the older NLR stock was soon to be encountered on workmen's trains in the North of England repainted in LNWR standard colours. Wolverton also constructed the trailer composites and driving trailers to match the electric motor units built by the Metropolitan Carriage, Wagon & Finance Company between 1914 and 1923. Utilizing electrical equipment supplied by the Oerlikon Company, these three car sets were popularly referred to as the 'Oerlikon Stock'. (See plate 40.) They led long useful lives, not being taken out of service until 1957–60. A 1915 motor coach is preserved in the National Collection, and is currently (1978) awaiting restoration.

The majority of the illustrations which follow are taken from a nearly complete collection of official North London Railway glass negatives (size 12 in by 10 in – 254 mm by 305 mm) which have been handed over by British Railways to the National Railway Museum following the 1968 Transport Act. They depict many aspects of operations on the NLR, and although some appeared in early volumes of *The Railway Magazine* (see the Select Bibliography), many others have probably never been published. Together they vividly illustrate the efficiency of a small railway enterprise and the pride of its staff in the Victorian and Edwardian eras.

C. P. Atkins
LIBRARIAN

T. J. Edgington
TECHNICAL INFORMATION OFFICER

National Railway Museum, York

SELECT BIBLIOGRAPHY

GENERAL

The North London Railway, by R. M. Robbins.
Originally published in 1937. A revised edition is still in print by the
Oakwood Press.

An illustrated interview with the NLR General Manager, G. B. Newton.
The Railway Magazine, September 1898.

An illustrated interview with the NLR Locomotive Superintendent,
H. J. Pryce.
The Railway Magazine, September 1900.

The North London Rail Route across the Capital, by G. Freeman Allen.
Trains Illustrated, March & May 1954.

The North London Line, by H. V. Borley and Charles E. Lee.
The Railway Magazine, February 1964.

BROAD STREET STATION

Chapter 5 of *London's Termini*, by A. A. Jackson, David & Charles,
1969.

London's Historic Railway Stations, by J. Betjeman and J. Gray,
John Murrary, 1972.

PASSENGER SERVICES

North London Railway Passenger Services, by J. F. Vickery.
Railways, January to October 1946.

TICKETS

The Tickets of the North London Railway, by H. V. Borley.
Journal of the Railway and Canal Historical Society, May 1962.

LOCOMOTIVES

Various issues of the *Locomotive, Railway Carriage & Wagon Review*
from September 1942 to August 1944 (anon).

Inside-cylinder 4-4-0Ts (51 class).
Journal of the Stephenson Locomotive Society, November 1939 (anon).

Outside-cylinder 4-4-0Ts (1 to 10 class).
Journal of the Stephenson Locomotive Society, March, May & July 1940
(anon).

Outside-cyclinder 0-6-0Ts (75 class).
Journal of the Stephenson Locomotive Society, August 1940 (anon).

A concise summary of all the locomotives built at Bow Works appears on
pp. 526–533 of *British Steam Locomotive Builders*, by J. W. Lowe,
Goose, 1975.

ROLLING STOCK

No historical account appears to have been published covering North
London Railway rolling stock.

SIGNALLING

The Railway Magazine, September 1906 (Broad Street only).

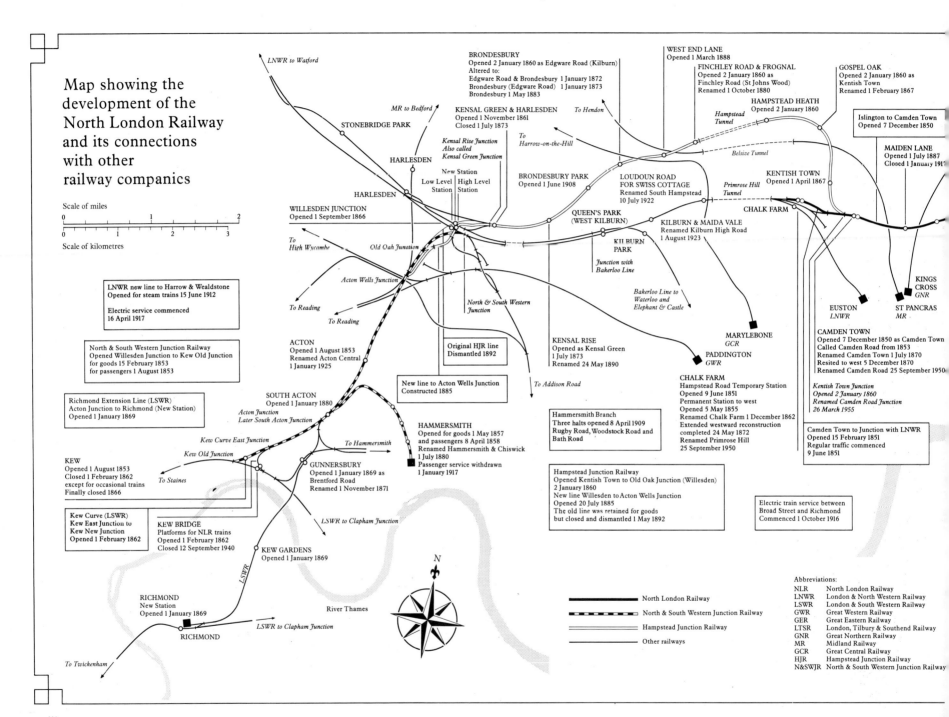

Map showing the
development of the
North London Railway
and its connections
with other
railway companies

Scale of miles

0   1   2

0   1   2   3

Scale of kilometres

LNWR to Watford

MR to Bedford

STONEBRIDGE PARK

HARLESDEN

HARLESDEN

*Kensal Rise Junction
Also called
Kensal Green Junction*

New Station
Low Level   High Level
Station   Station

WILLESDEN JUNCTION
Opened 1 September 1866

*To
High Wycombe*

Old Oak Junction

Acton Wells Junction

To Reading

To Reading

BRONDESBURY
Opened 2 January 1860 as Edgware Road (Kilburn)
Altered to:
Edgware Road & Brondesbury 1 January 1872
Brondesbury (Edgware Road) 1 January 1873
Brondesbury 1 May 1883

KENSAL GREEN & HARLESDEN
Opened 1 November 1861
Closed 1 July 1873

*To
Harrow-on-the-Hill*

BRONDESBURY PARK
Opened 1 June 1908

To Hendon

WEST END LANE
Opened 1 March 1888

FINCHLEY ROAD & FROGNAL
Opened 2 January 1860 as
Finchley Road (St Johns Wood)
Renamed 1 October 1880

HAMPSTEAD HEATH
Opened 2 January 1860

*Hampstead
Tunnel*

Belsize Tunnel

GOSPEL OAK
Opened 2 January 1860 as
Kentish Town
Renamed 1 February 1867

Islington to Camden Town
Opened 7 December 1850

MAIDEN LANE
Opened 1 July 1887
Closed 1 January 1917

LOUDOUN ROAD
FOR SWISS COTTAGE
Renamed South Hampstead
10 July 1922

KENTISH TOWN
Opened 1 April 1867

*Primrose Hill
Tunnel*

CHALK FARM

QUEEN'S PARK
(WEST KILBURN)

KILBURN & MAIDA VALE
Renamed Kilburn High Road
1 August 1923

KILBURN
PARK

*Junction with
Bakerloo Line*

*Bakerloo Line to
Waterloo and
Elephant & Castle*

*North & South Western
Junction*

KENSAL RISE
Opened as Kensal Green
1 July 1873
Renamed 24 May 1890

To Addison Road

MARYLEBONE
GCR

PADDINGTON
GWR

CHALK FARM
Hampstead Road Temporary Station
Opened 9 June 1851
Permanent Station to west
Opened 5 May 1855
Renamed Chalk Farm 1 December 1862
Extended westward reconstruction
completed 24 May 1872
Renamed Primrose Hill
25 September 1950

KINGS
CROSS
GNR

EUSTON
LNWR

ST PANCRAS
MR

CAMDEN TOWN
Opened 7 December 1850 as Camden Town
Called Camden Road from 1853
Renamed Camden Town 1 July 1870
Resited to west 5 December 1870
Renamed Camden Road 25 September 1950

*Kentish Town Junction
Opened 2 January 1860
Renamed Camden Road Junction
26 March 1955*

LNWR new line to Harrow & Wealdstone
Opened for steam trains 15 June 1912

Electric service commenced
16 April 1917

North & South Western Junction Railway
Opened Willesden Junction to Kew Old Junction
for goods 15 February 1853
for passengers 1 August 1853

Richmond Extension Line (LSWR)
Acton Junction to Richmond (New Station)
Opened 1 January 1869

ACTON
Opened 1 August 1853
Renamed Acton Central
1 January 1925

SOUTH ACTON
Opened 1 January 1880

*Acton Junction
Later South Acton Junction*

Original HJR line
Dismantled 1892

New line to Acton Wells Junction
Constructed 1885

Hammersmith Branch
Three halts opened 8 April 1909
Rugby Road, Woodstock Road and
Bath Road

Camden Town to Junction with LNWR
Opened 15 February 1851
Regular traffic commenced
9 June 1851

Kew Curve East Junction

Kew Old Junction

KEW
Opened 1 August 1853
Closed 1 February 1862
except for occasional trains
Finally closed 1866

To Staines

Kew Curve (LSWR)
Kew East Junction to
Kew New Junction
Opened 1 February 1862

KEW BRIDGE
Platforms for NLR trains
Opened 1 February 1862
Closed 12 September 1940

GUNNERSBURY
Opened 1 January 1869 as
Brentford Road
Renamed 1 November 1871

To Hammersmith

HAMMERSMITH
Opened for goods 1 May 1857
and passengers 8 April 1858
Renamed Hammersmith & Chiswick
1 July 1880
Passenger service withdrawn
1 January 1917

Hampstead Junction Railway
Opened Kentish Town to Old Oak Junction (Willesden)
2 January 1860
New line Willesden to Acton Wells Junction
Opened 20 July 1885
The old line was retained for goods
but closed and dismantled 1 May 1892

Electric train service between
Broad Street and Richmond
Commenced 1 October 1916

LSWR to Clapham Junction

KEW GARDENS
Opened 1 January 1869

N

River Thames

RICHMOND
New Station
Opened 1 January 1869

RICHMOND

LSWR to Clapham Junction

To Twickenham

LSWR

━━━━━━━ North London Railway

┅┅┅┅┅ North & South Western Junction Railway

═══════ Hampstead Junction Railway

─────── Other railways

Abbreviations:
NLR   North London Railway
LNWR   London & North Western Railway
LSWR   London & South Western Railway
GWR   Great Western Railway
GER   Great Eastern Railway
LTSR   London, Tilbury & Southend Railway
GNR   Great Northern Railway
MR   Midland Railway
GCR   Great Central Railway
HJR   Hampstead Junction Railway
N&SWJR   North & South Western Junction Railway

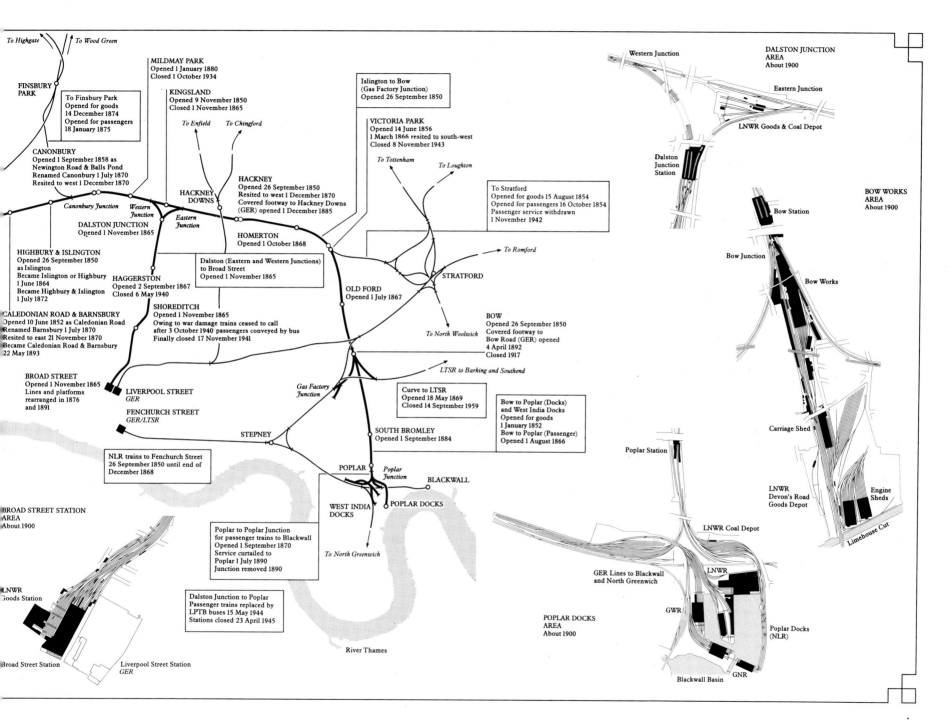

FINSBURY
PARK

To Highgate | To Wood Green

MILDMAY PARK
Opened 1 January 1880
Closed 1 October 1934

KINGSLAND
Opened 9 November 1850
Closed 1 November 1865

To Enfield | To Chingford

To Finsbury Park
Opened for goods
14 December 1874
Opened for passengers
18 January 1875

CANONBURY
Opened 1 September 1858 as
Newington Road & Balls Pond
Renamed Canonbury 1 July 1870
Resited to west 1 December 1870

Islington to Bow
(Gas Factory Junction)
Opened 26 September 1850

VICTORIA PARK
Opened 14 June 1856
1 March 1866 resited to south-west
Closed 8 November 1943

To Tottenham | To Loughton

HACKNEY
Opened 26 September 1850
Resited to west 1 December 1870
Covered footway to Hackney Downs
(GER) opened 1 December 1885

HACKNEY
DOWNS

Canonbury Junction | Western
Junction

Eastern
Junction

DALSTON JUNCTION
Opened 1 November 1865

HOMERTON
Opened 1 October 1868

To Romford

To Stratford
Opened for goods 15 August 1854
Opened for passengers 16 October 1854
Passenger service withdrawn
1 November 1942

HIGHBURY & ISLINGTON
Opened 26 September 1850
as Islington
Became Islington or Highbury
1 June 1864
Became Highbury & Islington
1 July 1872

HAGGERSTON
Opened 2 September 1867
Closed 6 May 1940

Dalston (Eastern and Western Junctions)
to Broad Street
Opened 1 November 1865

STRATFORD

OLD FORD
Opened 1 July 1867

CALEDONIAN ROAD & BARNSBURY
Opened 10 June 1852 as Caledonian Road
Renamed Barnsbury 1 July 1870
Resited to east 21 November 1870
Became Caledonian Road & Barnsbury
22 May 1893

SHOREDITCH
Opened 1 November 1865
Owing to war damage trains ceased to call
after 3 October 1940 passengers conveyed by bus
Finally closed 17 November 1941

To North Woolwich

BOW
Opened 26 September 1850
Covered footway to
Bow Road (GER) opened
4 April 1892
Closed 1917

LTSR to Barking and Southend

BROAD STREET
Opened 1 November 1865
Lines and platforms
rearranged in 1876
and 1891

LIVERPOOL STREET
GER

Gas Factory
Junction

Curve to LTSR
Opened 18 May 1869
Closed 14 September 1959

Bow to Poplar (Docks)
and West India Docks
Opened for goods
1 January 1852
Bow to Poplar (Passenger)
Opened 1 August 1866

FENCHURCH STREET
GER/LTSR

STEPNEY

SOUTH BROMLEY
Opened 1 September 1884

NLR trains to Fenchurch Street
26 September 1850 until end of
December 1868

POPLAR

Poplar
Junction

BLACKWALL

WEST INDIA
DOCKS

POPLAR DOCKS

Poplar to Poplar Junction
for passenger trains to Blackwall
Opened 1 September 1870
Service curtailed to
Poplar 1 July 1890
Junction removed 1890

To North Greenwich

Dalston Junction to Poplar
Passenger trains replaced by
LPTB buses 15 May 1944
Stations closed 23 April 1945

River Thames

BROAD STREET STATION
AREA
About 1900

LNWR
Goods Station

Broad Street Station

Liverpool Street Station
GER

Western Junction

DALSTON JUNCTION
AREA
About 1900

Eastern Junction

LNWR Goods & Coal Depot

Dalston
Junction
Station

BOW WORKS
AREA
About 1900

Bow Station

Bow Junction

Bow Works

Carriage Shed

LNWR
Devon's Road
Goods Depot

Engine
Sheds

Limehouse Cut

Poplar Station

GER Lines to Blackwall
and North Greenwich

LNWR Coal Depot

LNWR

GWR

POPLAR DOCKS
AREA
About 1900

Blackwall Basin

GNR

Poplar Docks
(NLR)

xix

1 Broad Street station frontage on Wednesday 29th June 1898. The additional entrance staircases and foot-bridges were added in 1890 and include some stained glass advertisements at the top of the stairs. There are circular carved monograms at the top of the building which have the initials NLR on the right and LNWR on the left. The City was very much a gentleman's preserve in late Victorian days. Only one lady is visible, carrying a parasol.

3 Broad Street station interior looking south from platform 8 before platform 9 was built outside the right hand wall.

The North London train in platform 8 was on the Kew Bridge or Richmond service. The LNWR coaches in platforms 5 and 6 were on the 'Outer Circle' service to Mansion House and carried roof boards, unusual elsewhere on purely local services, reading 'Broad Street, Willesden, Kensington and Mansion House. Change at Willesden for Main Line'. The small destination board under the eaves stated 'London and North Western Train'.

The North London brake van at platform 8 had fixed side and tail lamps, and four lamp irons, one of which carried a removable tail lamp. The North London coach on platform 5 was probably a service vehicle as it has end windows. A similar coach is illustrated in Plate 4. The man with the ladder was the station lamp man. Platforms 6 and 7 are surfaced with large York stone slabs.

2

2 The interior of Broad Street station on Monday 27th June 1898. Platforms 5 to 8 were normally reserved for LNWR trains and North London trains to Kew Bridge and Richmond. North London local trains and those to the GNR line used platforms 1 to 4. The ornamental partition on platforms 4 and 5 separated the two sections.

The LNWR train at platform 5 was on the 'Outer Circle' service to Mansion House (Metropolitan District Railway), a distance of $19\frac{1}{2}$ miles, although the two termini were only about $\frac{3}{4}$ mile apart. There is a North London train at platform 2. The pits between the rails were for the inspection of carriage underframes and brakegear, while the stand pipes were for replenishing gas containers in luggage vans.

The advertisements were an uncontrolled jumble, typical of the period, and there were even enamel plates advertising 'Pears Soap' on the platform edge. The station name was on the lamp glasses and this appeared to be the only means of identification. The train protection bars referred to in the text (p. xiii) can be seen fixed to the inner edge of the rail alongside platform 4.

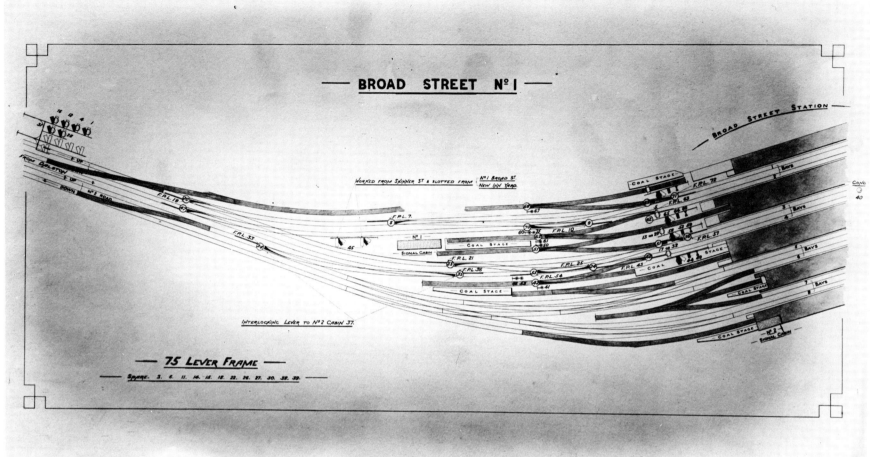

4 Broad Street station from the top of the water softening plant. The water tank and coal stage for servicing locomotives using platform 1 are in the foreground. The signals of LNWR design, controlling the entrance to the platforms, had the platform number painted on them. The signals for No. 1 lines had the LNWR type circle which indicated 'Slow Lines'.

The coach in the siding was probably a service vehicle as there is some descriptive lettering under the eaves and no class designation on the doors. The train in platform 4 was for Alexandra Palace and carries the GNR identification disc at the foot of the chimney.

5 The signal layout diagram for Broad Street No. 1 signal box, which controlled the approach to the station on No. 1 lines, and platforms 1 to 4. The locomotive sidings with coal and water facilities are clearly shown. There was one connection between Nos 1 and 2 lines, a facing cross-over from No. 2 up line to platforms 3 and 4.

7 A North London Railway 4-4-0T and close-coupled block train on the GNR main line near Hadley Wood in the early 1900s.

Photograph by C. Laundy, reproduced by kind permission of K. Leech.

6 Looking north from Broad Street, showing No. 1 signal box, and the west side of Liverpool Street station at a lower level on the right.

A train of nine LNWR 4-wheel coaches for the Mansion House service was in the siding at the right hand side of NLR viaduct, and a rush hour train of LNWR bogie stock for the Broad Street–Watford or Tring service on the left.

Apparently Stephenson Clarke & Co supplied some locomotive coal to the North London Railway, as two of their wagons are visible in the sidings.

The down line signals also had the line number painted on the arm, and the bracket signals to the left of No. 1 box read No. 2 and No. 2 to No. 1. These signals were controlled by Skinner Street box which can just be seen in the background.

8 North London Railway 4-4-0T No. 14, displaying on its chimney the route indicator for Richmond or Kew Bridge, heads a train bound for Richmond on the Hampstead Junction Railway, possibly leaving Finchley Road.
Photograph reproduced by kind permission of L. Ward.

9 Bow Junction in 1871. 4-4-0T No. 1, which appears to be brand new and which was built at Bow in that year, is on the left, and 2-4-0T No. 20, built by Sharp Stewart & Co in 1855, is in the foreground. No. 20, was probably acting as bank engine for trains to the Great Eastern line, and was withdrawn in 1871. The locomotive outside the shed is a 4-4-0T of No. 30 class built by Slaughter Gruning & Co in 1861. The coal wagon, although owned by the Hirwaun Coal & Iron Co also carried the words 'North London—Loco Department' and the coal may have been transported by sea from South Wales to Poplar.

FOLLOWING PAGES

10 Bow Junction in August 1893. The signal box appears to be the same building, slightly altered, as the one in plate 9. The Locomotive Works carry the date 'Rebuilt 1882'. The signals above the Locomotive Works, on a lattice post, apply to the curve from the London Tilbury Southend Railway to Bow Station NLR. The 'down' distant signal for Devons Road is attached to the walls of the works.

The bank engine siding in the right foreground appears to be disused.

11 Bow Junction on 9th July 1906. The Branch to the Great Eastern Railway diverges to the right, while the North London main line to Poplar runs straight ahead. Compared with plate 10, the distant signals for Devons Road are now on a separate post at the north end of the Works building. A new signal box has been built on the site of the box, in plate 10. The diamond and oval boards at the top of the steps indicated to the travelling linesmen whether their services were required at that box. The white side indicated that all apparatus was in order. When reversed, the red diamond and black oval, warned them that there was some defect at the box, and the services of a signal or telegraph linesman were required.

The signal box name was painted on the front of the box, and this appears to have been standard on the NLR, unlike most other companies which had either enamel plates or raised letters.

The bank engine siding has been removed, probably soon after the photograph in plate 10 was taken.

9

14 Bow Works Wheel Shop on 9th June 1898. The frame templates on the wall were for the 4-4-0Ts. The 6-ton walking-jib crane in the centre of the picture was driven by flying ropes. The wheels and axles on the right were for an 0-6-0T.

15 Bow Works Boiler Shop on 15th July 1903. The 10-ton electric overhead crane was built by Craven Brothers of Manchester in 1901. This view shows a plate bending machine on the left and a stamping machine in the centre, all belt-driven from overhead shafts.

By that time the boiler shop was lit by electric light.

12 Bow Works Locomotive Erecting Shop on 7th June 1898, with 4-4-0T No. 47 and 0-6-0Ts No. 75 and 77 on the left hand road. On the centre road are the frames for a 4-4-0T, frames and cylinders for 4-4-0T No. 4, another 4-4-0T, with two more locomotives behind it, while there are boilers on the right-hand side. The 30-ton capacity overhead crane, built by Craven Bros of Manchester, was driven by flying ropes.

No. 75 was the first of Mr Park's 0-6-0Ts built in 1879, and No. 77 was built in 1881. Both engines originally had stove-pipe chimneys and were painted in the green livery. This style was short-lived, the chimney soon being changed to the standard pattern and the livery altered to black.

13 Another walking crane in the forge at Bow Works, which appears to be moved by flying ropes but the lifting mechanism is hand operated.

14

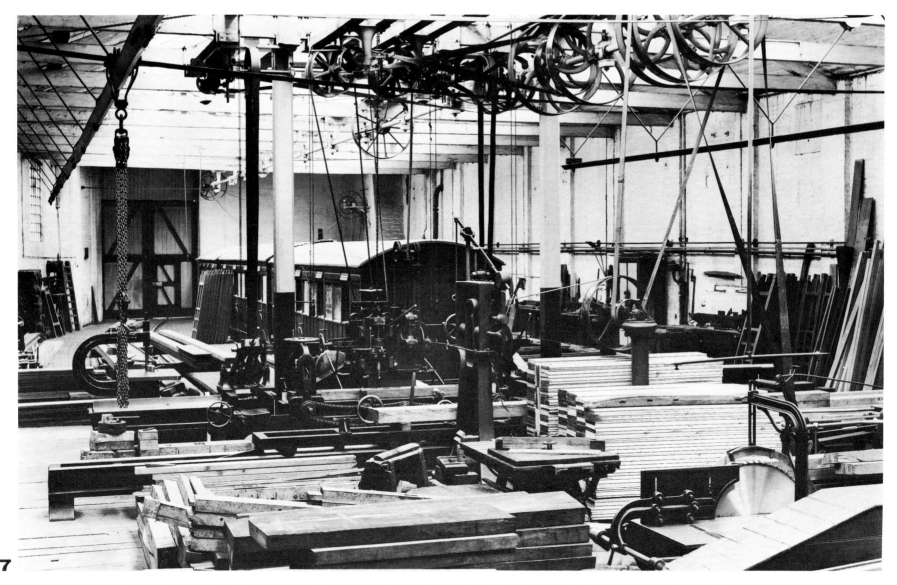

16   Bow Works Carriage and Wagon Shop. There were facilities for erecting forty coaches at one time, and standard underframes for goods rolling stock were also built here. The coaches of the passenger train on the left have had new roofs fitted with the centre lines 6 ins higher than those of the train on the right. The old stock on the right has the destination boards at waist level.

These were subsequently moved to below the cantrail as they could not be seen in the lower position from a crowded platform.

The lighting is by gas, with crude open batswing burners, a fire hazard in a building containing so much wood.

17   Bow Works Sawmills on 17th June 1898. Rough logs were received at one end of the mill, and they left at the other end as a finished coach body. Saws, drilling and planing machines are visible, all driven by belts from overhead shafting.

20

ON PREVIOUS PAGE

18 The Locomotive Superintendent's Office, Bow Works, on Saturday 5th July 1900. An interesting selection of locomotive photographs adorn the walls of Mr Pryce's office. Pride of place goes to a North London 4-4-0T, probably No. 88, over the fireplace, while below this are two GWR broad-gauge locomotives, *North Star* on the left and *Lord of the Isles* on the right. On the right hand wall are a number of prints depicting LNWR, Taff Vale, and GWR locomotives, and in the centre an American 'Camelback' 4-4-2 of the Lehigh Valley Railroad.

The antiquated telephone at the far side of Mr Pryce's desk was part of an internal system between the offices and the shop foreman. The exchange in the entrance lodge was operated by the gate porter.

19 Part of the Locomotive Superintendent's Offices at Bow Works on 5th July 1900. On the table in the foreground are results of tests carried out on samples of metal used in locomotive, carriage and wagon construction. The test room was at the end of the carriage fitting shop.

The model of 2-4-0T No. 17 in the glass case is now on display at the Science Museum, South Kensington. The framed photographs are mainly of North London subjects, but there is one of a Midland 4-2-2 above the model, and a Great Southern & Western Railway (Ireland) 4-4-0, possibly No. 301, below the NLR 4-4-0T. Mr Pryce received his training on the GS & WR before coming to the NLR.

20 4-4-0T No. 24, built by Robert Stephenson & Co in 1855. There were five locomotives in this class and all were withdrawn between 1868 and 1872. The driving wheels were flangeless and the caliper-type brakes operated on the rear pair of coupled wheels. The bogie was a very early type which rested on a central ball-shaped pivot and had no side play. The location is probably outside Bow Works.

21 4-4-0T No. 34 built by Slaughter Gruning & Co of Bristol in 1861 and here shown in original condition at Bow. No. 34 was sold in February 1882 to H. W. Lewis of Cardiff, on behalf of the Marquis of Bute, and was used for shunting at Cardiff Docks. Three of the other locomotives of this class were sold in 1886 to the Girvan & Portpatrick Junction Railway in South-West Scotland.

22

22 4-4-0T No. 43, designed by William Adams, was the first locomotive to be built at Bow Works in 1863. It is pictured here standing outside the old running shed at Bow, which was in 1882 rebuilt as the locomotive erecting shop. No. 43 was never rebuilt but was renumbered twice, first to 43A, and then to 101 in 1877, before being scrapped in 1888. As No. 101, it was the first NLR locomotive to be painted in black with red lining. The boiler pressure was 160 p.s.i. which was higher than contemporary pressures used by other railways. 140 p.s.i. was the usual figure in the 1860s.

23

23 4-4-0T No. 51, photographed outside Bow Works in its original condition, was the first NLR locomotive built with an Adams bogie. This engine enjoyed a long life, being built in 1865 and withdrawn by the LMS as late as 1925. It was renumbered 109 in 1885, and twice rebuilt, first at Bow in 1886, and then at the LNWR's Crewe Works in 1909. A cab was fitted at the first rebuilding. No. 109 was given a temporary LNWR number 2874, which was painted on the tank where the numberplate had been in 1922/3. The LMS number 6435 was allocated but never carried.

N.L.R. 108
REBUILT BY WORKS 1877

24

24 4-4-0T No. 108 was originally built at Bow Works in 1865 as No. 50 and was similar to No. 43 (plate 22). It is here shown as rebuilt in 1887, outside Devons Road shed on 27th August 1904. It was renumbered in 1884 and withdrawn from service in 1908. This class had a narrow cab fitted during Mr Park's superintendency, with the ejector placed outside the left-hand cab side sheet.

25 4-4-0T No. 113 at Devons Road on 6th May 1897. This was built in 1869 as No. 16 and was one of the first series of locomotives to be fitted with the Adams bogie (see plate 23). No. 16 was rebuilt at Bow in 1890 and was renumbered 113 in 1889, when the first No. 113 (formerly No. 55) was scrapped. It was withdrawn in 1910. This class had wider cabs than that on No. 108 (plate 24).

25

26   One of the earliest outside cylinder 4-4-0Ts No. 27, built at Bow in 1869. This photograph was probably taken at Bow when the locomotive was brand new. Various features which later disappeared figure prominently in this print; the number on the chimney, the sand box on top of the boiler, the long tail lever to the Ramsbottom safety valves, and a large capstan-like wheel for operating the hand brake.

27   The final development of the Adams outside-cylinder 4-4-0T appeared during Mr Pryce's term of office and is represented here by No. 88, photographed at Devons Road when new in June 1898. No. 88 was specially prepared for photography with wheels lined out and polished metal parts painted white. The front coupling is a three-link one normally used only on the 0-6-0T freight locomotives. Since the 4-4-0Ts ran bunker first for 50 per cent of their journeys, presumably the coach coupling was used with this locomotive, although other photographs of 4-4-0Ts show a screw coupling at the front. There is an old 10-ton goods brake van in the background, of the type partially shown in plate 45.

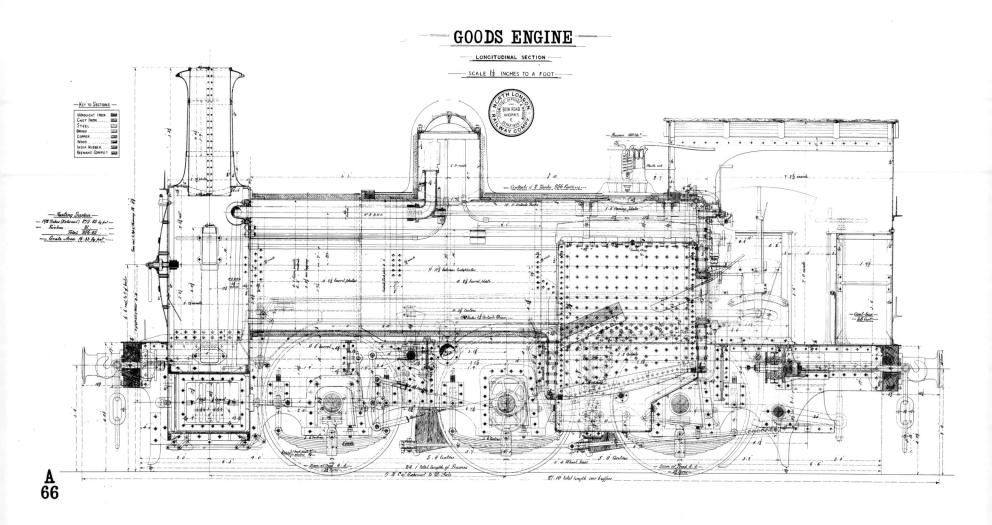

28 The General Arrangement elevation of a standard
North London Railway 0-6-0T.

GOODS ENGINE

TRANSVERSE SECTIONS

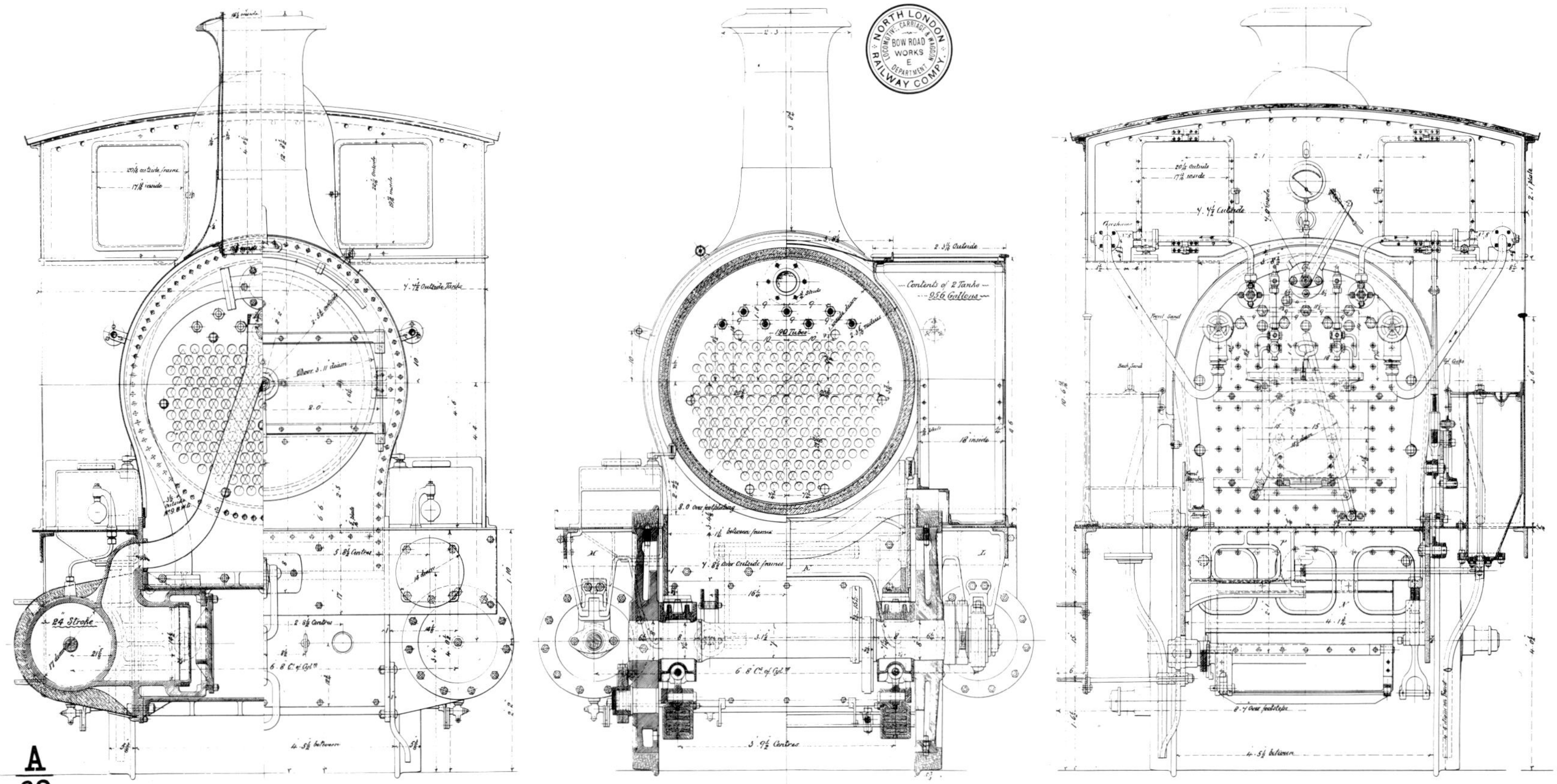

— SECTION THRO' SMOKE-BOX —   — FRONT END ELEVATION —

— SECTION AT LEADING AXLE —   — SECTION AT DRIVING AXLE —

— SECTION THRO' FOOTPLATE —   — SECTION THRO' TRAILING SAND-BOX —

SCALE 1½ INCHES TO A FOOT

A/68

N.E.R.
17
REBUILT BOW WORKS 1900

29

29 0-6-0T No. 17 built at Bow Works in 1889 and shown here as rebuilt in 1906. No. 17 was transferred to the LNWR after the working agreement of 1909 and became their No. 2877 and later LMS No. 7516, before being withdrawn in July 1932. This was a special livery for the photograph, as the 0-6-0Ts did not normally carry the 'coat of arms' when in service. These engines were capable of hauling large loads relative to their size, and on test at Harlesden a load of 699 tons, including the locomotive, was moved on a 1 in 100 gradient.

30 The Bow Works Steam Crane shown here as first rebuilt in 1872, with lengthened frames and an additional pair of carrying wheels. This locomotive was built as a conventional 0-4-0ST in 1858 by Sharp Stewart & Co for working the Hammersmith branch of the North & South Western Junction Railway. It was purchased by the North London Railway in 1859, and is seen here with Salter safety valves and no cab.

31 The Steam Crane as later rebuilt with a cab, wheels with 'H' section spokes, and Ramsbottom safety valves. During its life of over 90 years the steam crane was numbered successively 37, 29 and 29A by the North London Railway, 2896 by the LNWR, 7217 and 27217 by the LMS, and finally 58865 by British Railways. It was the oldest locomotive taken over by BR in 1948 and was scrapped in 1951.

32 4-4-0T No. 50 and a train of four-wheel coaches outside the carriage shed at Bow on 23rd July 1898. The coaches have raised roofs which contrast with the brake vans.

31

33 Four-wheel, four-compartment gas-lit first-class coach No. 99 built at Bow Works in 1906. All North London passenger trains were permanently close-coupled in sets, with short buffers at one end of the coach which fitted into concave brass-lined cups at the opposite end of the next vehicle. Safety bars were fitted across the drop light on all three classes of accommodation. The class was designated in words, and the NLR arms were displayed on each door. Smoking compartments were specifically labelled, but non-smoking accommodation has no positive indication.

34 Composite coach No. 19, a four-wheel five-compartment gas-lit vehicle for first- and second-class passengers, built at Bow Works in 1876. This coach has both classes of accommodation indicated in full, but the armorial device is only on the first-class doors. The second-class has a monogram of the initials NLR.

33

34

35 Second-class coach No.114 built at Bow Works in 1905, four-wheel, five-compartment, gas-lit. Smoking was permitted in all the compartments, so it appears that there was no non-smoking accommodation for second- or third-class passengers. The underframes for all coaches and passenger vans were built to the same design and the wood used was teak. The class designation is in words and the monogram is on the door panel.

36 Four-wheel five-compartment third-class coach No. 194 built at Bow Works in 1903. This is an all-smoking coach and there are no partitions between the compartments, thus allowing itinerant buskers to entertain a whole coach. Three lamps were provided for the five compartments and the only upholstery was narrow strips laid on the wooden seats without springs or padding. The class designation is shown in both words and figures.

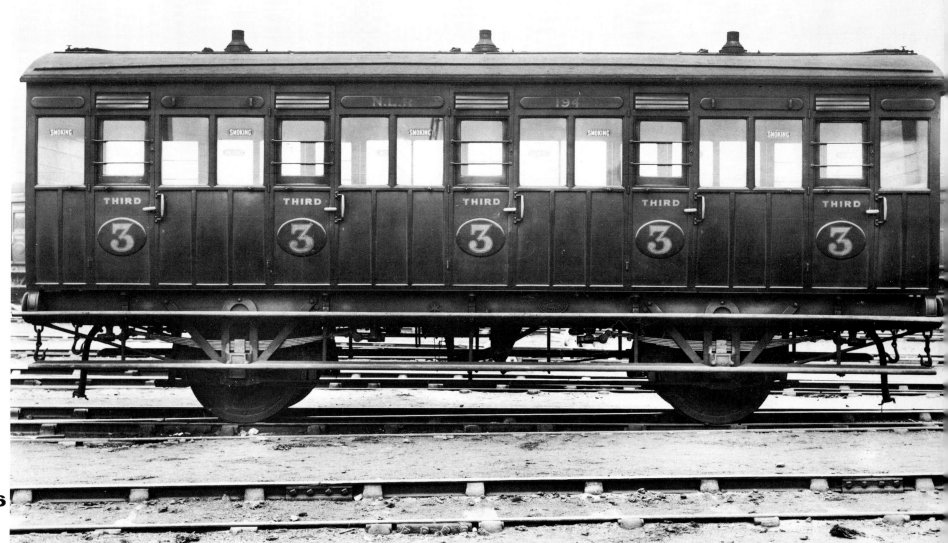

N. L. R.

LUGGAGE VAN. No 100

GUARD'S COMP!

37

37 Four-wheeled luggage and guards van No. 100, built at Bow in 1902, with a raised lookout for the guard. Vans were always marshalled at the ends of trains and had normal length buffers at the outer end with screw couplings. These ends of the vans were painted red. A large gas container was installed in the inner end of the van, connected by pipes along the roofs of all coaches to the carriage lighting. This was later replaced by individual pressure cylinders on each coach. In some of the vans two third-class compartments were then constructed in the space that had been occupied by the gas container. The guard's compartment has no outside door lock handles. This was a safety precaution to avoid the guard being shut out after giving the right away. One door, the righthand one in this photograph, swung outward, but was normally kept bolted. The other door swung inwards and could only be secured with a non-slam lock from inside the van. There was a dog box at the outer end of the van with two small ventilated doors.

38 North London Railway directors' saloon No. 32, built in 1872, here shown as preserved in the National Railway Museum. This was built on a standard underframe, but has full-length buffers at both ends. The saloon was renumbered 1032 by the LNWR, the number it now carries, and was allocated the number 45003 by the LMS in 1933. The door panels were originally oval and carried the company's 'coat of arms'. The centre saloon contains two tables and four fixed settees. One end compartment is a lavatory and the other a pantry for the service of refreshments.

39   Four-wheel five-compartment second-class coach No. 122, built by the LNWR for the North London Railway at Wolverton in 1910. Unlike earlier vehicles illustrated, two of the compartments are not labelled for smokers. These trains were marshalled in two five-coach close-coupled sets as follows: Brake Third/third/first/first/and second. Second/first/third/third/and brake third. The buffers were of the short type between all coaches, except at the outer ends of the brake thirds and the inner ends of the seconds in the middle of the train. The two types can be clearly seen in this picture.

Reproduced by kind permission of the Oxford Publishing Company.

40   An LNWR electric motor-coach introduced on the Broad Street–Richmond service in 1916. The electrical equipment was supplied by Maschinenfabrik Oerlikon, of Switzerland, and the coach was built by the Metropolitan Carriage Wagon & Finance Company, of Birmingham. The intermediate and driving trailers were built by the LNWR at Wolverton.

The vehicle illustrated, No. 31E, is now in the reserve collection at the National Railway Museum. It was renumbered No. 5751 by the LMS and in 1933 it became No. 28249. This was the last working 3-car 'Oerlikon' set, being used as depot shunter at Stonebridge Park Carriage Shed until 1963. The last set to run in traffic was in April 1960, on the Watford–Croxley Green branch. In busy periods two trains were coupled together to form a six-car unit.

41 10-ton Locomotive Coal wagon built in 1894 at Bow Works, described on the works plate as 'Bow Road'. Only one brake block acts on each pair of wheels and these are operated by a lever on one side of the wagon only. Earlier wagons had a single brake operating on one wheel. Like the carriages, all the wagons were built on a standard underframe except certain specialized vehicles similar to the trolley illustrated in plate 44.
The photograph was taken on 19th June 1894.

42 A standard 10-ton wagon being lifted by hand-operated sheerlegs outside Bow Works on 19th June 1894. This clearly shows the construction of the wagon's frame, the single-sided brake, and the rubber pads on the buffers and drawgear.

41

42

43 A four-wheel well wagon of 10 tons capacity built at Bow in 1903, and used by the Locomotive Department at Bow Works for the conveyance of components and stores within the Works, and possibly to Devons Road Locomotive Depot. It was photographed on 21st August 1905, probably at Devons Road, and shows a large reserve stock of coal neatly stacked in the background.

44 Bow Works Workmen's Cab as rebuilt in 1899, photographed on 21st August 1905, probably at Devons Road.

43

45 10-ton Goods Brake Van No. 18 built at Bow Works and photographed there on 10th May 1898 when brand new. Part of one of the older design of brake vans is visible on the left. The signals on the curve from the London Tilbury & Southend Railway to Bow Station can be seen above the van (see also plate 10). The outside rigging to the brake blocks is unusual.

46 The result of a collision at Devons Road signal box on 12th March 1900. The locomotive No. 46 was hauling the 9.30 pm Poplar to Broad Street when at about 9.35 pm it collided with an empty coal train from Lea Cut to Poplar. Twenty eight passengers and six staff were slightly injured. The mishap was due to a lapse of memory and irregular working by the signalman at Devons Road, who allowed the empty coal train to shunt into the section towards Bow Junction on the down line without first offering it to the signalman there on the block instruments. The damaged locomotive and wagon appear to have been shunted into the carriage shed clear of the main lines.

47 4-4-0T No. 49 in the Locomotive Erecting Shop doorway at Bow Works showing damage to buffer beam and front end of frames. The date and details of the mishap are not known. The locomotive still has a three-link coupling at the front.

48 The North London Railway's docks at Poplar looking west and showing the London & North Western Railway's goods shed on the middle arm of the dock with the GWR warehouse behind. The GNR also owned a goods depot at Poplar, off the picture on the left. The GNR possessed running powers over the North London to Poplar, but the GWR did not enjoy this facility and their traffic was worked by North London engines.

The docks and goods depots covered an area of 28 acres and there were 14 miles of sidings. All the waterborne traffic in the North London Company's docks appears to have been conveyed by lighters and sailing barges. The sea-going sailing vessel in the background is in the West India Import Dock.

There is a notice on the wall in the foreground directing people to Poplar station, there described as East India Road. The four moveable coaling cranes in the foreground were introduced about 1895 by Mr Pryce.

49 Poplar Dock on 15th December 1893, showing three 15-cwt fixed coal derricks. These were all worked by hydraulic power, as was most of the handling equipment in the dock. In 1898 this comprised seventy-three cranes and hoists, forty capstans, eight coal tipplers and a swing bridge. The hydraulic power was generated by six pairs of compound steam pumping engines delivering against four accumulators loaded to 700 p.s.i. Steam was supplied by six locomotive-type boilers working at a pressure of 160 p.s.i.

50 Poplar Dock on 22nd June 1898, showing a hydraulic coal tippler for discharging end-door wagons. The wagon, owned by Wm. Cory & Son Ltd, a large firm of coal merchants in London, is a typical 8-ton vehicle with dumb buffers, and side and end doors. The hand brake is on one side of the wagon only, operating two large wooden brake blocks. A row of capstans for shunting the wagons is visible on the right.

With the relatively long exposure needed, this photograph shows how the coal dust blew about, even on a fine summer day.

51 Another view of Poplar Dock on 22nd June 1898, showing a side-discharge wagon on a hydraulic tip. This vehicle, owned by the Staffordshire Chemical Company, who had private sidings connecting with the North Staffordshire Railway at Chatterley, probably conveyed coke rather than coal, as it has a removable extension above the normal wagon body to carry an equivalent weight of coke, which is less dense. This wagon has spring buffers but it still retains the single-sided brake.

49

51

52 4-4-0T No. 40 with a group of drivers outside South Acton Locomotive Shed.

53 Another group of North London officers and staff posing in front of 4-4-0T No. 60 at Devons Road in about 1904. The officer tenth from the right can also be seen eighth from the right in the frontispiece, but looking some-what younger! In this group no top hats are in evidence but three "gentlemen" are wearing straw boaters.

A scale model of this locomotive, No. 60, was built at Bow Works. After many years on display at Broad Street station, it is now at the National Railway Museum.

54   A group of guards posing in front of inside-cylinder
4-4-0T No. 109, outside Devons Road Locomotive Shed.
The builder's plate is just visible on the driving wheel
splasher.

55 An unknown celebration in Bow Works. The central
shield above the dais depicts the gateway of the West India
Dock which appears in the North London's armorial
device.

WELCOME
NORTH LONDON RAILWAY
NORTH LONDON RY
NORTH LONDON RAILWAY
OPENING
BLACKWALL
TUNNEL
MANCHESTER
AND
ALL STATIONS ON THE
LONDON
NORTH LONDON
STAINES & WINDSOR
THAMES RIVER SIDE
BURNHAM BEECHES
NORTH LONDON RAILWAY
FLOWER SHOW
TEMPLE GARDENS
GOODS & PARCELS
ROYAL MAIL ROUTE
SCOTLAND
ENGLAND & IRELAND

56 Poplar Station decorated for the opening of the Blackwall Tunnel by HRH the Prince of Wales, on Saturday 22nd May 1897. There is a poster on the second board from the left advertising this event, and exhorting people to book to Poplar station and travel by North London Railway. The other posters advertise excursions to Windsor, the Royal Horticultural Society's Annual Flower Show in Temple Gardens, and LNWR services to Scotland and Ireland.

INDEX

Plate numbers are set in **bold** type.

Printed in England for Her Majesty's Stationery Office by Format (Haywards Heath) Ltd.
Dd 587531 K48